A New Hc … nity

Sheila Hollins … …atchinson
and David Towell
illustrated by Beth Webb

Beyond Words

London

1

3

6

7

13

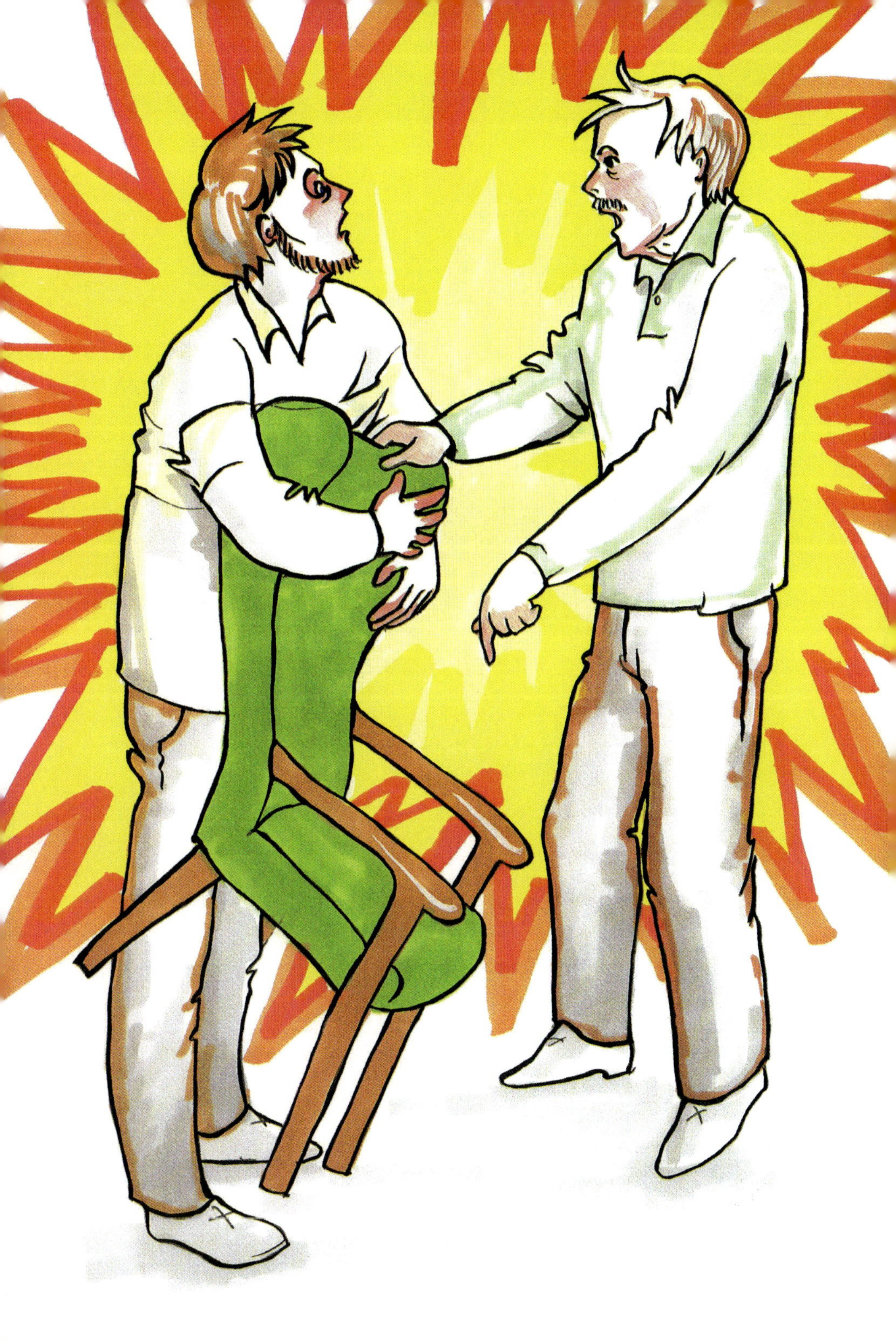

15

VAO 386

17

VAO 386

19

23

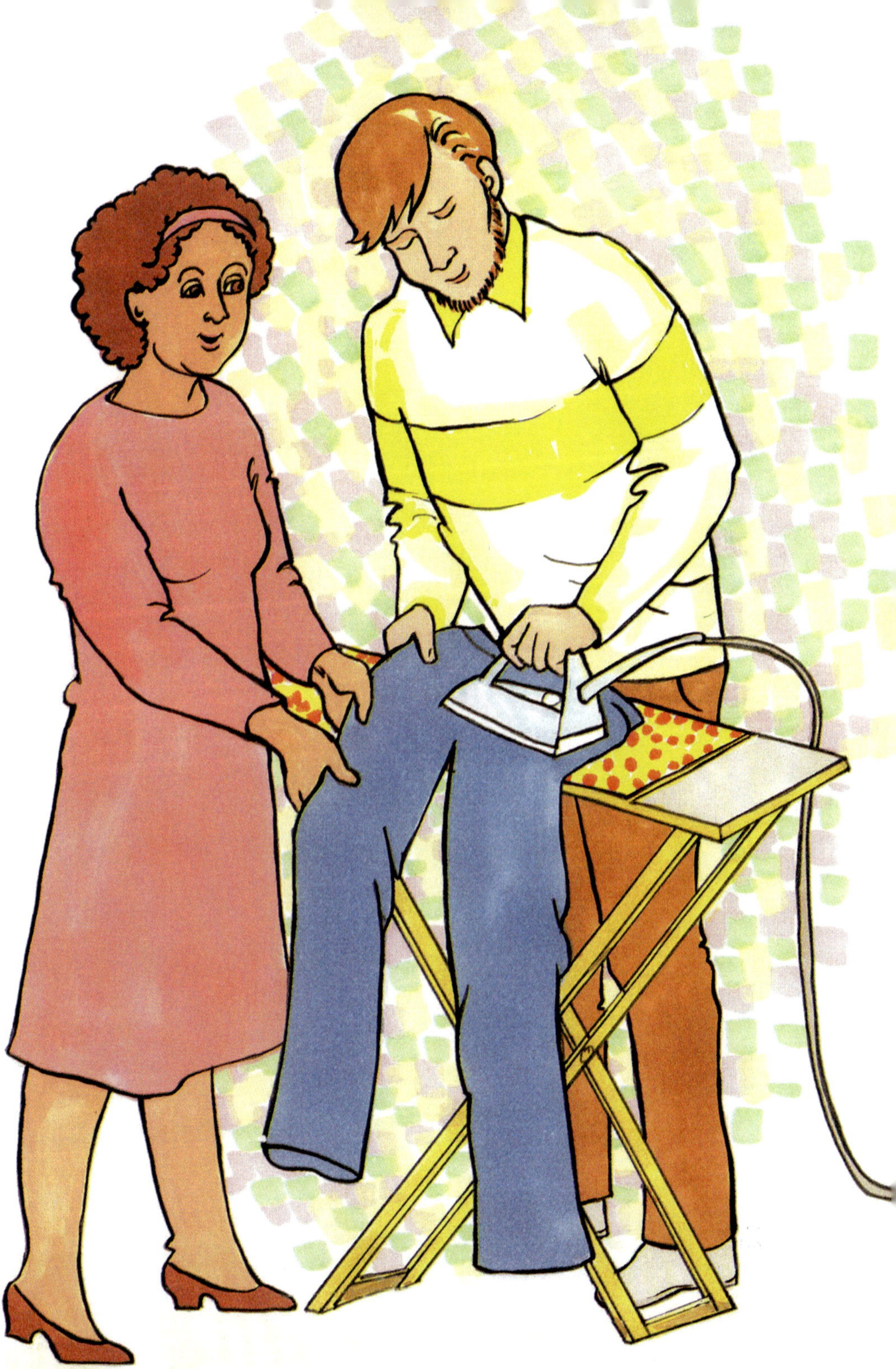

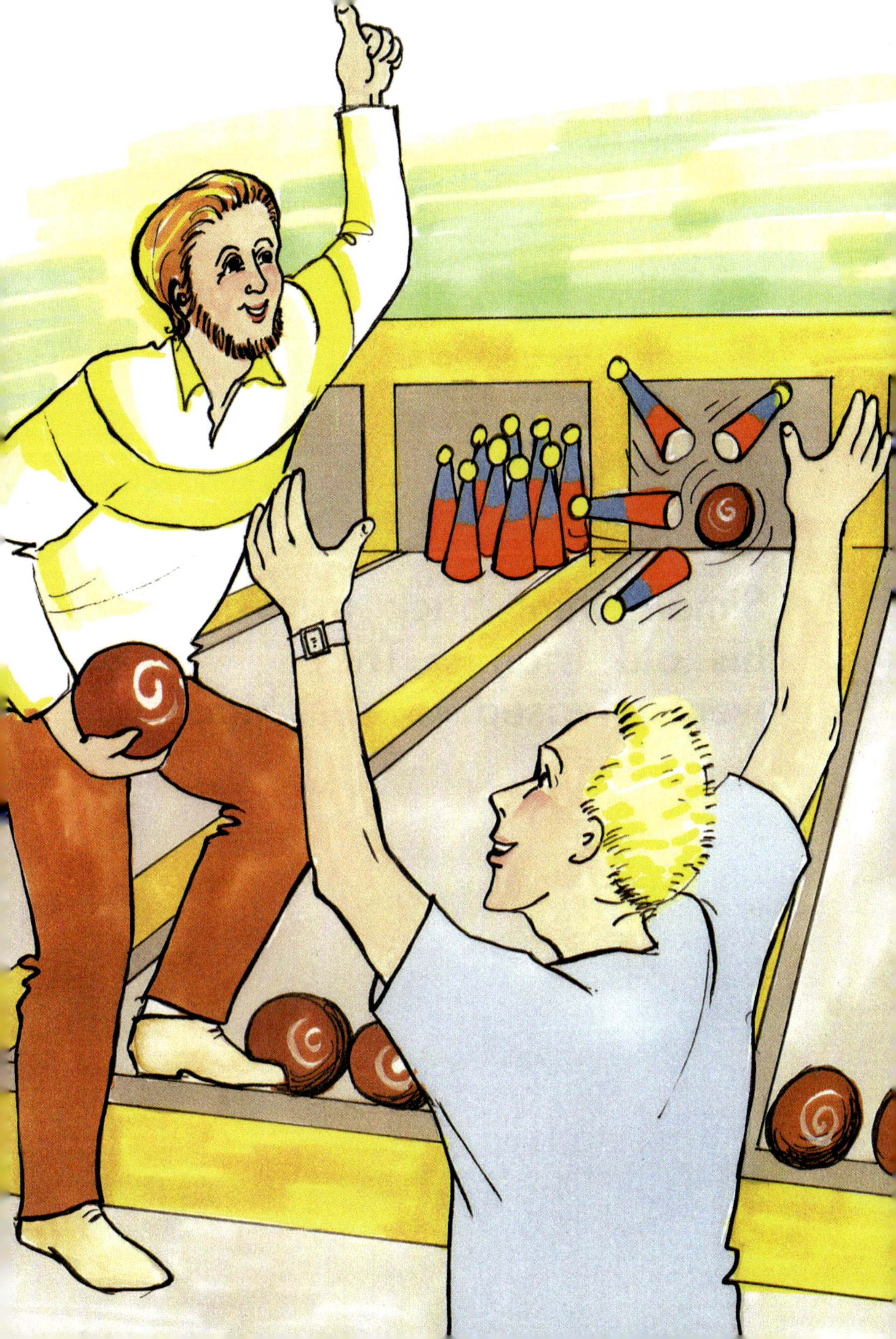

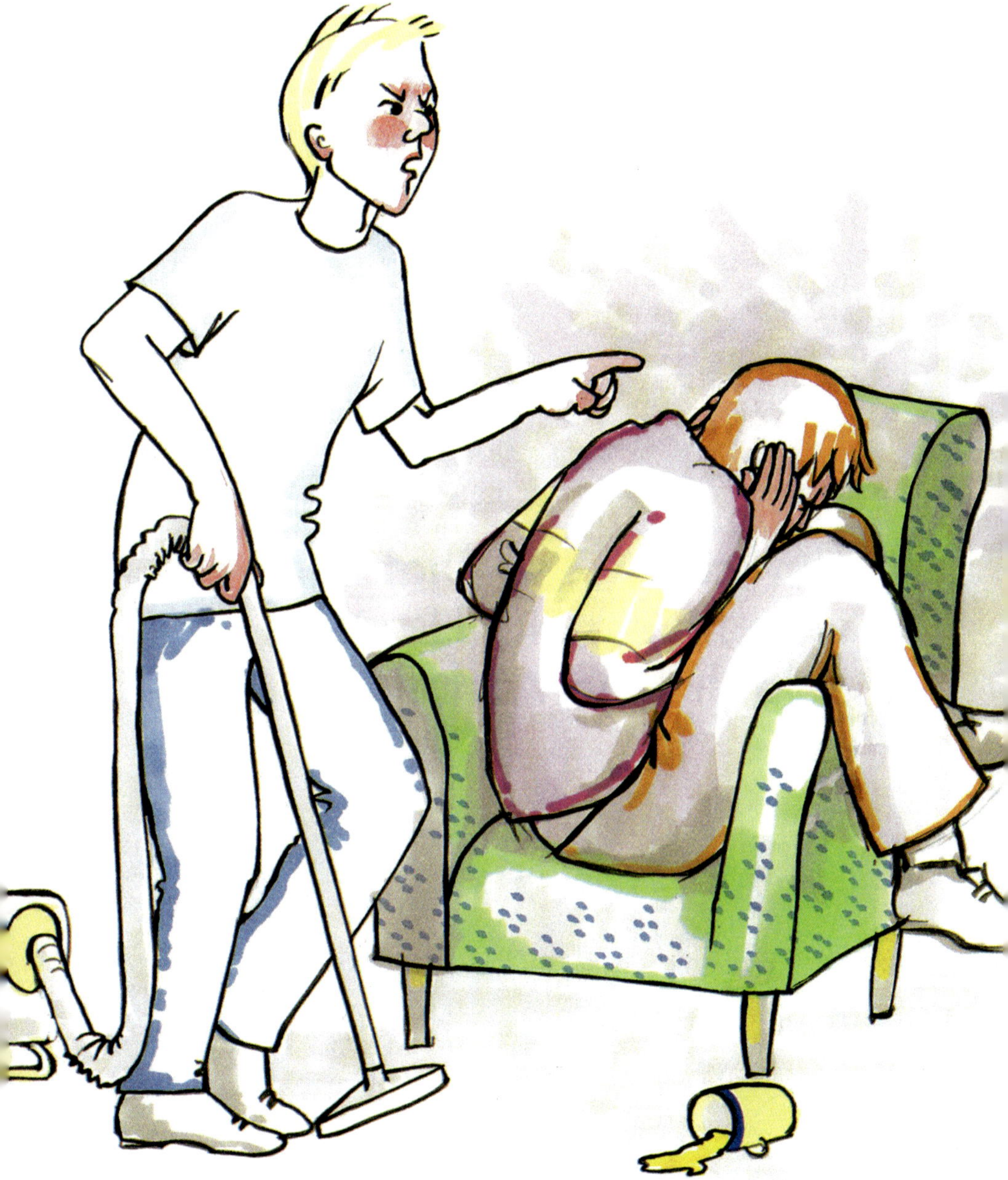

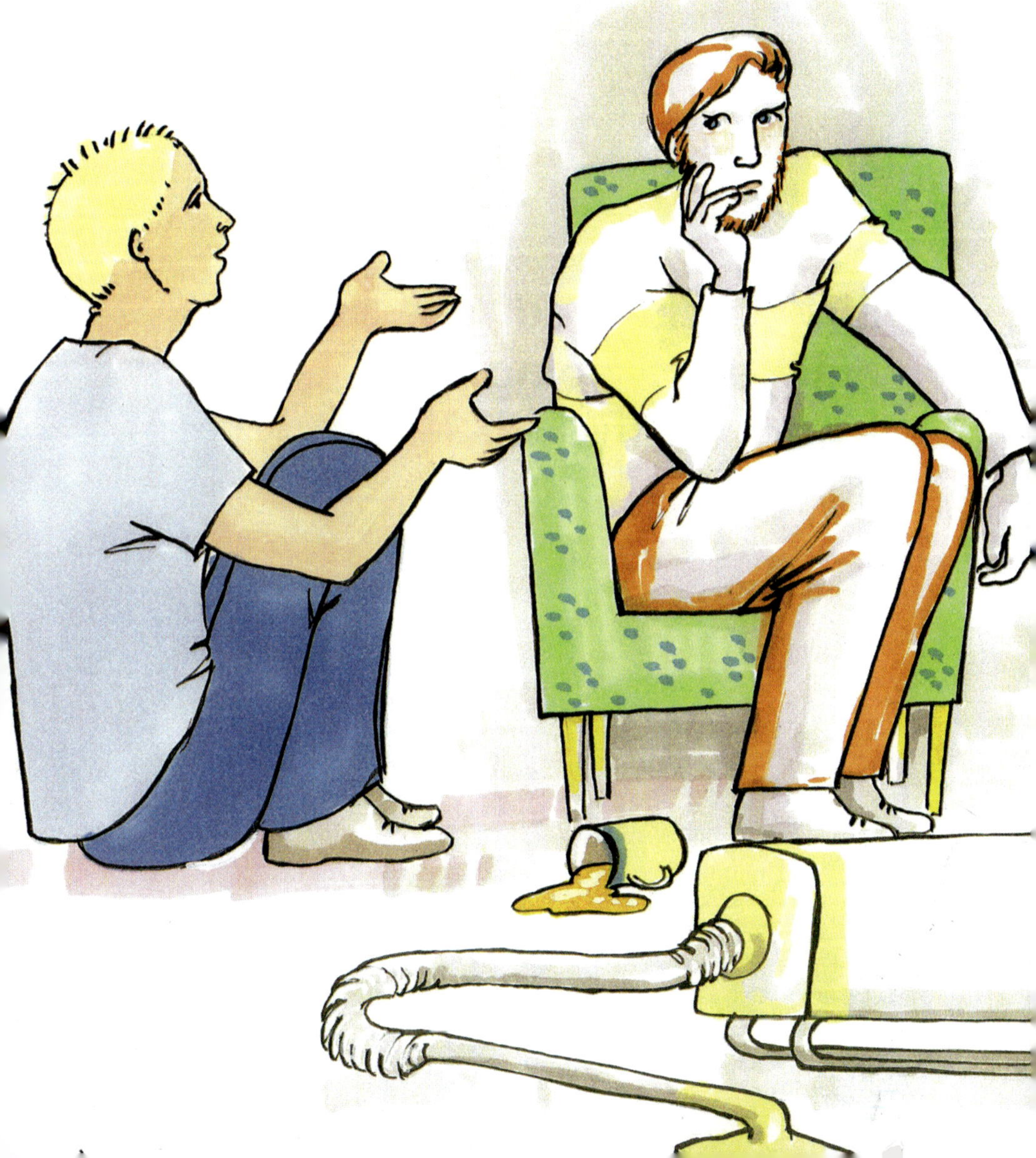

First published 1993 by St George's Mental Health Library.

Second edition published 2015 by Books Beyond Words.

ISBN 978-1-78458-052-0

British Library Cataloguing-in-Publication Data
A catalogue record for this book is available from the British Library.

Printed by DX Imaging, Watford.

Books Beyond Words is a Community Interest Company registered in England and Wales (7557861).

St George's Hospital Charity is a registered charity (no. 241527).

Contents

Storyline

The following words are provided for readers and supporters who want some ideas about one possible story. Most readers make their own story up from the pictures.

1. Stephen lives here with some of his friends.

2. His social worker tells him about a new house. "Do you want to come and see it?" she asks.

3. Stephen goes to see the house.

4. Mary, Tim, Linda and Jo live there. He likes them a lot.

5. Stephen gets a letter. The letter says Stephen can move to the house. He feels excited.

6. But Stephen thinks about his friends and carers. He likes them too.

7. Stephen thinks about the people in the new house, Mary, Tim, Linda and Jo.

8. Stephen talks to his carers. He asks what to do.

9. Stephen talks to his social worker about the new house. He says, "I want to move out. I want to move to this house."

10. Stephen's social worker talks to her bosses at social services. They say the new house is OK.

11. Stephen and his social worker talk about when he can move.

12. Stephen packs his things. He feels sad about leaving.

13. Stephen wants to take his chair. One of his carers says, "No!"

14. Another carer says, "It's Stephen's chair. If he wants to take it, he can."

15. Stephen gives presents to his friends. They give him presents too, and a picture. They say, "Come and see us soon."

16. Stephen feels nervous when he gets to his new home.

17. They carry his things inside.

18. The chair is very heavy. It is hard work getting it upstairs!

19. Stephen feels happy and proud when his room is ready.

20. At dinner everyone talks to Stephen.

21. At bedtime Stephen can't sleep. Now he feels sad and lonely.

22. Next day Stephen is a bit quiet. Mary tries to cheer him up with some coffee. She sees his broken picture.

23. Mary helps Stephen feel at home.

24. Later he enjoys shopping with Linda.

25. Another day Stephen goes bowling with Tim. They have a wonderful time.

26. Stephen goes back to visit his old friends. They are so pleased to see him.

27. They give him a cup of tea. Stephen tells them about his new life.

28. Stephen feels confused when it is time to say goodbye.

29. Stephen walks home slowly. He doesn't want to go in.

30. He won't help Tim with the jobs. Tim gets cross when Stephen knocks a mug over.

31. Tim can see that Stephen is missing his old life. He tries to help his new friend.

32. Stephen cheers up. He enjoys helping Tim and Linda in the kitchen.

33. When the jobs are done, they all have fun together.

34. Now Stephen lives here, with Mary, Tim, Linda and Jo.

What happens when people move home?

Stephen's story is a good one. He is successful in moving out from the large home (sometimes called an institution) where he lived, and moving into a new house which he shares with other people. But the pictures don't cover all the different stages involved in deciding about moving.

Reading the pictures in this book can start a conversation about moving home, and supporters and carers can help people develop their ideas by continuing that conversation in different ways. Sometimes this will be a conversation just involving one person who is thinking about moving. Sometimes it will be even better if a small group is involved, most or all of whom are thinking about how their future lives could be different. For some people circles of support may be helpful. These are groups of friends and supporters who are involved in a person's life and want to help them plan and make goals for their future, including plans for where and how they want to live. Circles of support meet regularly to work on helping the person achieve their goals.

The conversation would need to happen slowly to build up the idea of moving, with good communication at each stage about anything that people are anxious about, giving them the opportunity and support to rethink initial plans. This is about each person making choices for themselves. It will be important to maintain the parts of their life that help them feel safe, for example day activities, social outings or seeing family, so that they do not worry that moving will disrupt everything.

This will mean working with the person on their plan to establish what people and things they want to stay in their life, and making sure this happens.

There are lots of ways to help each person understand the options available to them, including pictures, videos, magazines and websites. In the story the main character only visits one place where he could live; in practice a person may want to visit a few different places before deciding what they like. They could visit other people who have moved home and see what it's like for them. Perhaps they could stay over for a night or two.

Planning for a move will include thinking how someone will decorate and furnish their new room or home, and who they would like to help them.

Plans also must be made for the support each person wants and needs. What does this person want and need help with? A local authority assessment may be needed to decide how much money is available to support the person. It's wise to start working with new support workers or managers before the move.

Stephen's experience

Moving isn't easy for Stephen. To start with he is sad about leaving his familiar home, and 'homesick' in his new home. And he has to learn a lot about getting on with other people and doing more for himself.

Often people like Stephen who have lived in an institutional setting for a long time don't have much choice. When moving is suggested to him, Stephen has lots to think about. For example: is this the right time to move out? He also has to sort out lots of practical things with the help of the people who know him best. How do you find a good place? Do you want to live on your own or with other people? Do you need some support to live the life you want to? How do you get the money to pay for this?

These seem like difficult questions and they are, but we all have to face them. The first time we moved was probably the hardest, especially if it involved moving from our family home. (In Stephen's case this may have been especially hard because he moved into an institution.) But we will all probably move again – perhaps several times – as we get older. Maybe we will meet someone we would like to live with. Maybe we will get a job in another town and want to move closer to where we work. And if we are not happy with where we live, we may want to think about all this again.

Lots of people have found good answers to the questions above. Many others are still looking for the best answer for them. There are organisations that will help you. The notes which follow discuss these questions in a little more detail, and tell you about some of the information and some of the organisations that could help you find a home. We have used examples from England but similar things exist in most other rich countries.

Everyone needs a home

What does it mean to have a home of your own?

Paradigm is an organisation that gives information about good support. They have tried to answer this question using 11 short sentences:

- I choose who I live with
- I choose where I live
- I have my own home
- I choose how I am supported
- I choose who supports me
- I get good support
- I choose my friends and relationships
- I choose how to be healthy and safe
- I choose how I am part of my community
- I have the same rights and responsibilities as other citizens
- I get help to make changes in my life

Why is a home of your own so important?

Of course, home is where you live and everyone has to live somewhere! (Otherwise we say that they are 'homeless'.) But home is more than this. Home is where you 'feel at home'. This means you feel comfortable, safe and secure. It also means that you feel that it is your home.

We are all different and like to live in different ways: some of us like to live in a city, some of us like to live in the country; some of us like lots of people around us, some of us like our own space; some of us like to live near family, some of us like to live near our friends; and some of us just like to try different things.

The United Nations says that every person with a learning disability, like every other person, has the right to live independently and to be included in their community.

We choose a place we like. We have furniture and decorations which we choose – remember Stephen wanting to take his chair. This is all our stuff. We can show visitors what kind of people we are by the posters on our walls, the music we play, the food we cook. And it's somewhere we can invite our friends. Come round to my place! It's also somewhere which has a front door, and where you have your own front door key. You decide who comes in.

In this story, Stephen wasn't living with his family. Perhaps his parents had died or were sick. Most countries now try to find a family for every child but there are still some children and young people who have grown up in children's homes. Not living in a family can make people feel sad. But it is still hard to make a change from a life which is familiar. Like Stephen, there comes a time when most of us want a home of our own. This tells other people: we are adults now and want to be in charge of our own lives.

Some people who grew up with their families were admitted to a hospital or home because of their own health problems, or because of their parents' health problems. Perhaps that happened to you. When it is time to leave the hospital you may be able to choose whether to go home to your family or to begin a new more independent life. If your family are involved in your life, you can ask them to help you think about where you will live. We will think more about making decisions in a minute

Moving home

Just because home is so important to us, moving home can be exciting but it can also be difficult, as it is for Stephen. Moving home means moving out and moving in. Stephen moves in to share a home with some other people. There are lots of good things in this. Stephen feels more grown up. He gets the first place of his own, sharing with other people. He is more 'in charge' of his life. He gains some new friends and starts doing new things with them (like going bowling).

But big changes are never easy. Stephen misses people in his past life, although he is able to visit them from time to time. He gets some new friends but has to learn how to get on with them around the house and do his share of the housework. When people live together, there is always the chance of getting into an argument. Just like on TV programmes (like Hollyoaks or Eastenders in the UK)!

But this is life for all of us. Stephen has to learn how to cope with these new experiences, and he is lucky that his new friends help him when times are difficult.

Finding a good place to live

There are lots of practical things to decide about when moving home. There are lots of different possibilities. Let's list some of them.

Where do you want to live?

It could be a flat or a house (or perhaps even a houseboat, although not many of us do this).

Do you want to live on your own or with other people?

It could be with just one other person or maybe with two or three. You may want to live with friends you already know from school or somewhere else.

Does your home need to have special adaptations?

There are many adaptations, alarms and devices that can help you live more independently.

Do you want to rent your home or buy it?

If you rent your home (for example from a private landlord, council or a housing association) you will be a tenant. You can also borrow the money to buy a home, or part of it. If you buy your home you will be an owner but of course, you will need to have ways to pay the money you have borrowed back, usually over many years. You can get advice about these different choices.

Stephen is in contact with a social worker who looks out for possibilities which might suit him and knows about how local councils can arrange the money. Local councils also give housing advice to anyone looking for a place and know, for example, about council housing and housing offered by housing associations. And there are usually estate agents in the high street who know about places to buy and places to rent from private landlords.

There are also organisations that work all over the country to help people find a home that suits them. See the Useful resources section.

Deciding for yourself

Whoever advises you on moving must help you to make the decision. They should not just make the decision for you. In England and Wales the Mental Capacity Act (2005) says that you must be supported to make decisions about your life for yourself, for example by getting information in a form that you can understand. This book has been designed to help you to make a decision about where you want to live.

If the decision is too difficult for you, then someone you know – perhaps a family member – can be involved in deciding what is in your best interests. If you don't have a relative or friend who can help, in England and Wales an Independent Mental Capacity Advocate (IMCA) can be appointed by social services to set up a best interest meeting. How to do this is laid down in guidance about the Mental Capacity Act. If you cannot decide for yourself, sometimes the Court of Protection will be asked to decide where you will live.

The story in this book can also be used to help social workers or other professionals assess how much help you need to make a decision to move home.

Getting the support to live as you want to

Some of us will be able to get on with our lives relying only on our family, friends and people we live with. Others will need more help, in practical things like managing money and paying the bills, in daily activities like dressing or cooking or using public transport, in things which affect our health like taking our medicines or visiting our doctor, or maybe when we feel worried or lonely, or need help to get on with our neighbours and housemates. Of course some people with learning and other disabilities may need a lot of support, even someone staying in their home all night in case they have a problem.

In Stephen's case, his social worker knew about who provides the kind of support he needed close to where he decided to live. The social worker also worked out how much the local council (or perhaps another public agency like the health service) would pay for this, depending on how much support Stephen needs. For all of us, the local council has a duty to help if we need it, although they may not offer us as much money or help as we want.

In England some people like Stephen will be able to get a budget for their support (sometimes called 'Direct Payments', 'Individualised Funding' or 'Personal Budget') and be able to hire a support worker directly. Even if you don't have a budget, you should still be involved in deciding who you want to support you. Some independent organisations know a lot about this and employ staff who provide support. These organisations also know about how to find a place to live.

If you are moving home you will probably want to find out about some of these organisations, what they could offer and of course whether you like the look of this! See the Useful resources section.

What is good support?

One of the most important questions we need to answer in moving home is: who will provide us with good support and what will this involve?

Paradigm's 11 statements give one definition of good support. Some organisations that employ support workers offer their own definition. The Care Quality Commission is a national agency in the UK which sets standards for support, inspects the organisations that provide it and writes reports about their inspections which are available to the public.

Most simply, we will want support which values each of us as a person, helps us to live our lives safely and in the ways we want, and empowers us to be active members of our local community.

Our home is more than a place to live: it is also the base from which we live our lives outside the home, getting to know other local people, making friendships, joining in activities we like and making a contribution (for example, through work, volunteering or just being a good neighbour) to community life.

Useful resources

Services in the UK

Social service departments

Local authority social service departments manage and purchase social care, for example, housing and day services for people with learning disabilities. If a person is moving into a new home, a social worker or care manager will carry out an assessment to see what support they need. This support may be part-funded by the local authority and part by the person themselves, depending on how much money they have.

Housing and Support Alliance

The Housing and Support Alliance is an independent advice and information service for people with learning disabilities and their families. They give advice on all issues relating to housing, support and rights for people with learning disabilities. They specialise in advice about housing options that enable people with learning disabilities to have more control over where and how they live. In particular they can help with ownership options and the various ways that people can invest in housing for family members who have a disability. They have a comprehensive website, including an easy read section featuring videos and picture stories to help people make choices. Their telephone advice service is available for members, people with learning disabilities and their families.
Telephone advice service: 0300 201 0455 or 0845 456 1497, 9am–4pm, Monday to Friday.
www.housingandsupport.org.uk

Housing Options Scotland

Housing Options Scotland offers housing advice and information for people with disabilities in Scotland, aiming to ensure that all people have access to affordable housing that meets their needs. The website includes information on benefits and sources of financial help for homeseekers with disabilities.
www.housingoptionsscotland.org.uk

Paradigm

Paradigm is a training and development agency offering support and resources to help people, communities and services to focus on people's needs and aspirations to live ordinary lives. The website has a lot of information, including videos and stories of action.
www.paradigm-uk.org

Care Quality Commission (CQC)

The CQC is a public agency responsible for registering and inspecting all health and social care providers in England. On the website you can find information about their standards and reports about specific providers. You can also contact the CQC if you have any concerns about the quality of support you or someone you know is receiving.
National customer service centre: 03000 616 161
www.cqc.org.uk

The Mencap Learning Disability Helpline

The Learning Disability Helpline is an advice and information service for people with learning disabilities, their families and carers. It also provides information and advice to anyone wanting to know about learning disability issues and services. The Helpline can advise

on a wide range of issues including community care, housing and money.
0808 808 1111

The **Foundation for People with Learning Disabilities** provide some information about the benefit of circles of support for people with learning disabilities, as well as help to get started.
www.learningdisabilities.org.uk/our-work/familyfriends-community/circles-of-support/

Written resources

National Development Team for Inclusion (NDTi)
The NDTi has produced a number of reports, looking at improving how people with disabilities find a home and the support they get to live as they choose.
My Own Place. Practical tools and advice for young people with disabilities and their families.
www.ndti.org.uk/publications/ndti-publications/my-own-housing/
Making the Move. A guide for people planning and managing housing and support services for people with learning disabilities.
www.ndti.org.uk/publications/ndti-insights/insights-1-making-themove/
The Real Tenancy Test. A simple test to review whether or not a supported living service is working in the right way and helping people to live how they choose. The report includes information about different types of tenancies, and protecting people's rights in line with the Mental Capacity Act (2005).
www.ndti.org.uk/publications/ndti-insights/insights-2-the-realtenancy-test/

Reach: Support for living an ordinary life
Produced by **Paradigm**, Reach is a resource pack and a set of standards for providing individualised support to people in supported living. The pack comes in two parts: *It's My Life*, mainly aimed at people with learning disabilities, their family and supporters, which can be bought on its own; and the *Service Review Pack*, mainly aimed at service providers and commissioners. To order, contact Paradigm on: 020 8870 8643 or email: jeanetteg@paradigm-uk.org

Raising our Sights. How-to guide 5: Housing
A guide produced by the **PMLD Network** in association with **Mencap**, looking at issues in providing housing for people with profound and multiple learning disabilities (PMLD). The guide includes a summary of housing options available, the law that protects people's rights, a pathway to accessing housing, and routes to challenging authorities who do not provide appropriate housing and support.
www.mencap.org.uk/sites/default/files/documents/2012.340%20Raising%20our%20sights_Housing_V3.pdf

Housing Learning and Improvement Network (**LIN**) factsheets
Housing LIN is an information resource primarily aimed at commissioners and providers of housing and care services for older people. The website has a set of factsheets on housing provision and mental capacity.
www.housinglin.org.uk/Topics/browse/Housing/Personalisation/?parent=3695&child=1940

Related titles in the Books Beyond Words series

Peter's New Home (2014, 2nd edition) by Sheila Hollins, Deborah Hutchinson and David Towell, illustrated by Beth Webb. Peter faces the hard decision of leaving his family for a group home. Not only does he miss his mum and dad but he has to start doing things for himself for the first time. Peter discovers that his new friends are there to help.

George Gets Smart (2001) by Sheila Hollins, Margaret Flynn and Philippa Russell, illustrated by Catherine Brighton. George's life changes when he learns how to keep clean and smart. People no longer avoid being with him and he enjoys the company of his work mates and friends.

Michelle Finds a Voice (1997) by Sheila Hollins and Sarah Barnett, illustrated by Denise Redmond. Michelle has cerebral palsy and cannot communicate what she is feeling to the people who might help her. Michelle and her carers explore various solutions to overcome these difficulties, including the use of signing, symbol charts and electronic communication.

Falling in Love (1999) by Sheila Hollins, Wendy Perez and Adam Abdelnoor, illustrated by Beth Webb. This love story follows the relationship between Mike and Janet from their first date through to deciding to become engaged to be married.

Authors and artist

Sheila Hollins is Emeritus Professor of Psychiatry of Disability at St George's, University of London, and sits in the House of Lords. She is a past President of the Royal College of Psychiatrists and of the BMA, and chairs the BMA's Board of Science. She is founding editor, author and Executive Chair of Books Beyond Words, and a family carer for her son who has a learning disability.

Deborah Hutchinson was a psychiatrist working with people with learning disabilities at a time when large numbers were moving from long-stay institutions into the community. Her personal experience was that she had to move home many times as a child.

David Towell is Director of the Centre for Inclusive Futures. He is best known for his leadership role in the King's Fund 'An Ordinary Life' initiative which helped to transform thinking about the opportunities and support available to people with learning disabilities and prefigured Valuing People.

Beth Webb is an artist with a background in psychology and sociology who specialised in alternative communication media. She has pioneered the use of emotional colour and mime in her illustrations for the Books Beyond Words series.

Acknowledgments

With grateful thanks to Freda Macey, Anita Conroy, Jennifer Pearson, Emily Westlake, the Special Trustees of St George's Hospital, and many others whose help and encouragement has made this book possible.

Beyond Words: publications and training

Books Beyond Words will help family carers, support workers and professionals working with people who find pictures easier than words for understanding their world. A list of all Beyond Words publications, including Books Beyond Words titles, and where to buy them, can be found on our website:

www.booksbeyondwords.co.uk

Workshops about using Books Beyond Words are provided regularly in London, or can be arranged in other localities on request. Self-advocates are welcome. For information about forthcoming workshops see our website or contact us:

email: admin@booksbeyondwords.co.uk
tel: 020 8725 5512

Video clips showing our books being read are also on our website and YouTube channel: www.youtube.com/user/booksbeyondwords and on our DVD, *How to Use Books Beyond Words*.

How to read this book

There is no right or wrong way to read this book. Remember it is not necessary to be able to read the words.

1. Some people are not used to reading books. Start at the beginning and read the story in each picture. Encourage the reader to hold the book themselves and to turn the pages at their own pace.

2. Whether you are reading the book with one person or with a group, encourage them to tell the story in their own words. You will discover what each person thinks is happening, what they already know, and how they feel. You may think something different is happening in the pictures yourself, but that doesn't matter. Wait to see if their ideas change as the story develops. Don't challenge the reader(s) or suggest their ideas are wrong.

3. Some pictures may be more difficult to understand. It can help to prompt the people you are supporting, for example:

- Who do you think that is?
- What is happening?
- What is he or she doing now?
- How is he or she feeling?
- Do you feel like that? Has it happened to you/ your friend/ your family?

4. You don't have to read the whole book in one sitting. Allow people enough time to follow the pictures at their own pace.

5. Some people will not be able to follow the story, but they may be able to understand some of the pictures. Stay a little longer with the pictures that interest them.